IMAGES
*of America*

# GIANT CITY STATE PARK

Among the first to carve his name into the stone walls along Giant City Boulevard was Albert Thompson, shortly after he returned home to Makanda from the Civil War at the age of 19. The carving states, "Of Ill., Albert S. Thompson, Fremont Body Guard, February 27, 1862 A.D." Since then, hundreds more names have been etched into the sandstone. (Courtesy of Jackson County Historical Society.)

ON THE COVER: This couple appears in a series of promotional photographs for Giant City State Park, taken by a Springfield, Illinois, studio for use by the Illinois Department of Parks (now Illinois Department of Natural Resources). Here they are exploring the Giant City Nature Trail, where visitors can walk the "streets" of Giant City and see firsthand how the park earned its name. (Giant City State Park, Illinois Department of Natural Resources.)

IMAGES
*of America*

# GIANT CITY STATE PARK

Karen Sisulak Binder

ARCADIA
PUBLISHING

Published by Arcadia Publishing
Charleston, South Carolina


Library of Congress Control Number: 2010920405

For all general information contact Arcadia Publishing at:
Telephone 843-853-2070
Fax 843-853-0044
E-mail sales@arcadiapublishing.com
For customer service and orders:
Toll-Free 1-888-313-2665

Visit us on the Internet at www.arcadiapublishing.com

*This work is dedicated to the memory of Col. Joshua Thompson
and his family, including those who settled between Makanda
and Carbondale as Thompsons, Stotlars, and Sisulaks.*

# CONTENTS

# ACKNOWLEDGMENTS

There are many people who helped make this collection possible. They include: Giant City State Park staff, particularly park superintendent Bob Martin and Michael Crawley; Ken Cochrane and Bob Morefield at the Jackson County Historical Society in Murphysboro for their deft maneuvering around centuries of information; Civilian Conservation Corpsman Earl W. Dickey for sharing his Camp Stone Fort experience at Giant City, as well as highlights from his remarkable 94 years of life; the Kelley family, especially Richard Kelley as a generous host and gifted storyteller, Mike Kelley as a fun boss, fellow Terrier, and a knowledgeable guide to lodge lore; Jim Boozoitis for the countless conversations under those hallowed arches; Kristin Stotlar Sisulak, my mother, for helping me find the roots of our family tree; and Steve Binder, my husband, who helped me blaze a trail through the park history and whittle my words along the way.

Most of the material for this book was drawn from information prepared by the Illinois Department of Natural Resources available at the Giant City Visitor Center in Makanda, Illinois. Unless otherwise noted, all images are courtesy of the Giant City State Park, Illinois Department of Natural Resources.

# INTRODUCTION

Giant City has some of best-traveled streets in the Midwest. Even before the park property was bought by the state of Illinois in 1927, the curious walked through its unique geology, residents picnicked on the bluffs, naturalists studied the flora of Fern Rock, and Civil War renegades hid among the bluffs. Today the Illinois Department of Natural Resources says that more than 1.2 million people a year visit the 4,055-acre park in Jackson and Union Counties, 12 miles south of Carbondale in deep southern Illinois.

This book's photographs travel through highlights in Giant City State Park history from various perspectives and are far from a complete accounting. There is Albert Thompson, a Civil War soldier from Makanda who etched his place in park history in 1862, and Earl W. Dickey, a Civilian Conservation Corpsman with Camp Stone Fort until 1935. And despite its massive stone structure, the lodge has become a warm and welcoming dining destination by its concessionaires, including Richard and Mike Kelley, a father-son team who celebrate their 30th season at the lodge in 2010.

Thompson was the son of Col. Joshua Thompson, who settled in Makanda in 1852. While Albert was home from a stint with the Fremont Body Guard, he etched his name on the stone wall face along Giant City Avenue. Yet it was as young boys at the beginning of the Civil War that Albert and his brother, T. W., joined with others at their father's farm, Banner Hill, to raise an American flag on top of a poplar tree, waving their support of the Union.

Albert went on to build a farm and orchard on the east ridge above the bustling railroad town of Makanda, and even served as station master there for 12 years. His brother, T. W., settled about 10 miles north on a Carbondale farm, which he later donated to what is today Southern Illinois University. The campus is full of places named after the Thompsons, including the woods and lake, offering places for thousands to visit, including the author, T. W.'s great-great-grandniece.

The role of the park in Dickey's life was circular. As a young man from central Illinois, he enrolled in the Civilian Conservation Corps (CCC) to save money for tuition. His CCC work first had him encamped at Giant City and then in Wisconsin before going to college in Michigan and seminary in New York. Although most of his pastoring was done in central Illinois, he did serve as clergy for the United Methodist Church in nearby Murphysboro. When the federal government opened up lands around Little Grassy and Devil's Kitchen lakes for recreational development by non-profit interests (such as churches, Scouts, and SIUC's Touch of Nature), he helped establish the Little Grassy Methodist Camp on Giant City Road, just up the road from the park.

Dickey was happily assigned next to the pastorate in Newton, near his hometown of Wayne City in central Illinois. He was the minister there from 1979 to 1999, and retired to the Makanda area, closer to his grandchildren and great-grandchildren. He now lives a half-mile from the church camp he helped start and a mile from the state park he helped build. At the age of 94, he still visits the Giant City Visitor Center every Friday afternoon, an idea suggested by his wife, Juanita, shortly after they retired to southern Illinois.

Richard and Mike Kelley's work at the lodge is a true family affair. Besides these two, Richard's wife, Kaye, graces the hostess station every weekend night, and Richard's son-in-law, Jim Boozoitis, is one of the managers. On big Sundays, such as Easter or Mother's Day, the entire family and more join forces. Just as the fried chicken dinner is a Sunday tradition for many families, it is too for the Kelleys. Every Sunday afternoon, after the church crowds thin, the clan gathers for a late afternoon dinner.

Most people visit the park for fun, and it is the intent of this collection to offer interesting insights into the park with a twist of fun through vintage and retro photographs. This is by no means an academic treatment nor a complete historical account. It is intended as a souvenir of memories from Giant City State Park.

# One

# SANDSTONE AND SHALE

Giant City State Park immerses visitors in natural and scenic beauty as told by the park's namesake geology and forest habitat. Yet these rocks and woods are crisscrossed with man's footprints, ranging from the Stone Fort, a Late Woodland American Indian site dated from 600 to 800 A.D. and the woods hiding Civil War renegades in the 1860s, to the roads laid in the 1930s by the Civilian Conservation Corps (CCC) legions.

This juxtaposition of nature and man is the bedrock for Giant City State Park's unique story. Beginning 300 million years ago, the park was a low plains area of the ancient Gulf of Mexico that drained into a sandy delta area south of the park. As the earth compacted, it created the sandstone and shale that is prevalent throughout deep southern Illinois. About 270 million years ago, the process of uplift and fracturing within the sedimentary rock layer heaved gargantuan ends of the bedrock to the Earth's surface and formed the small range of hills punctuated with occasional bluffs that generally cross the region. The land went from sea level to elevations between 350 and 1,000 feet high, exposing the sandstone layers to weathering conditions. The wind and water worked around the stone, easily cutting strange shapes from the softer sandstone and gouging channels around the denser, iron-laced sandstone layers that appear reddish.

The bluff faces also were weathered by sun exposure. Those with southerly faces received more radiant heat, which warmed the rock and evaporated moisture more quickly. These conditions created a dry microclimate on top of these bluffs, where prickly pear cactus, huckleberry, red cedar, and other dry soil plants can be found.

Perhaps the most dramatic geologic event for the park was roughly 20,000 years ago. A late Pleistocene glacier stopped 1.5 miles north of the Giant City State Park boundaries. The resulting Ice Age melt eroded and shifted blocks of rock into more shapes and formations, which visitors can see today.

Some unique photographs in this chapter were taken by Robert Farmer, a newspaper editor and photographer from Tamaroa, Illinois. Farmer's images are interesting not only because they were taken before the CCC camps, but because they are images taken with a camera using glass negatives. Farmer was known to have traveled the countryside on weekends. He also took what were known as "penny pictures" of people, quick snapshot cameo photographs that were popular at the time.

The chapter closes with a collection of pictures from the last private landowner of the park, Willis Rendleman.

Giant City State Park's strange and unique geology has been its top attraction since before it was protected as a state park. The earliest settlers in the area were mostly farmers looking for land to clear. One man in particular, Daniel Coleman, enjoyed the hunting enough that he eventually settled in 1803 along Drury Creek to be as close as possible to the unusual geological features. Among these visitors was photographer Robert Farmer of Tamaroa, who made souvenir photographs of sightseers on a camera using glass negatives. His handwritten titles on some of the images appear in the lower right corners. (Courtesy of Jackson County Historical Society.)

It was nature, not man, that created the vertical walls along Giant City Avenue. Two types of rocks make up the park's bluffs. On top is a layer of soft shale called Drury shale, while the lower layer is medium-grain sandstone called Makanda sandstone. The waters from the glacial melt about 20,000 years ago cut away first at the soft shale and then eroded the harder sandstone more slowly.

A trick of nature, slow erosion allowed massive blocks of stone to break apart in a consistent, uniform manner. This is why the rock walls are so vertical, and in some cases, some of the turns are near perfect right angles around the corners.

Another creation of glacial melt, Devil's Standtable captures visitors' imaginations immediately. Although the origin of the name is not known, this freestanding stone pillar also has been called the mushroom rock, but many thought it conjured the image of a massive pulpit for the devil. The devil theme pops up throughout the region: Devil's Kitchen Lake (which was once known as Devil's Well), Devil's Backbone, Devil's Whirlpool, Devil's Bake Oven and Devil's Half Acre. The origin of these names is now lost to memory.

While the park has been noted for its natural beauty, the geological interests rank first, noted *Outdoor Illinois* magazine in 1962. "A group of huge blocks of sandstone, made up of arrangements that resemble city blocks and streets, give the park its name. These have perpendicular walls that in some places are so perfect they seem man made and are so awe-inspiring in their size and shape that one is spellbound by their strangeness," the article stated.

With Southern Illinois Normal University 12 miles north, naturalists and other academics discovered the park's bounty of unique flora and fauna. A flower called French's Shooting Star and Synandra mint were discovered on the same day in the area known as "Fern Rocks" by Dr. George Hazen French. Not 100 feet from French's discovery of the shooting star, Stephen Forbes found the Forbes' saxifrage.

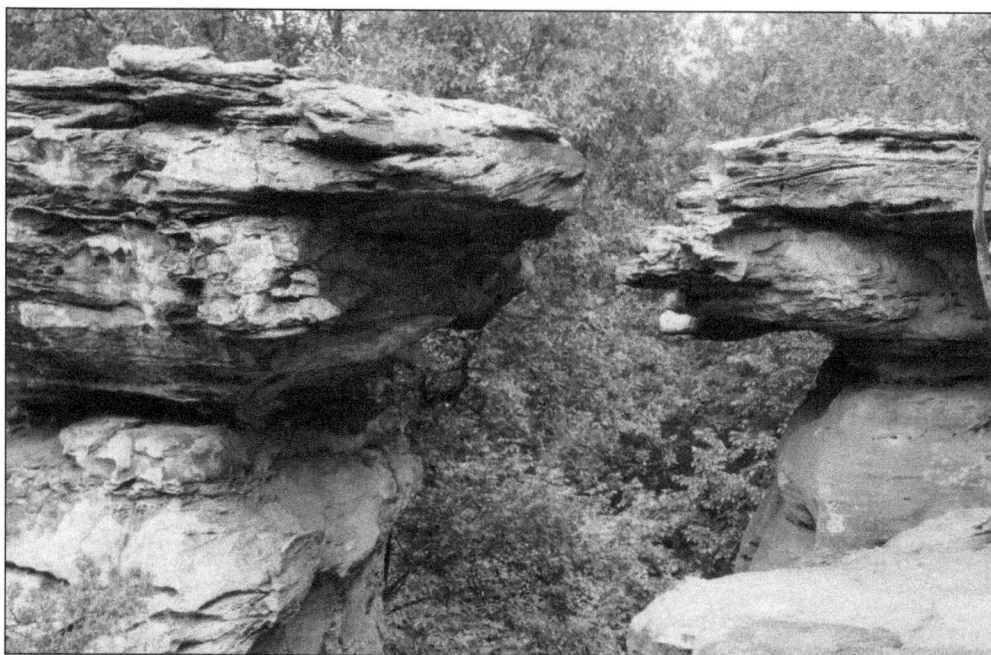

It is believed that Devil's Standtable was created when a large chunk of the neighboring bluff cracked loose as the region's hills were formed. As winds and rains washed away the softer materials from the stone block, the resulting formation left a column of sandstone topped with a cap containing sandstone with a higher content of iron.

A *St. Louis Post-Dispatch* reporter gave this poetic description of the park's geology in a travel article: "Pockmarked from being flogged through the ages by the wind, the rocks are warriors that have seen a time the rest of us may only wonder about."

It is believed this balanced rock was jostled from above during an earthquake and slid downhill into its current position, wedged and held in place by its own weight. It is possible that another earthquake could be strong enough to move it yet again. The New Madrid Fault is within 100 miles of the park and is the largest seismic zone in the country outside of the west coast. (Courtesy of Jackson County Historical Society.)

Students, teachers, and researchers have been studying Giant City's offerings since before it became an official state park in 1927. Naturalists from the nearby Southern Illinois Normal College (predecessor to the Southern Illinois University Carbondale located north of the park), started studying the flora and fauna shortly after the college was founded in 1869.

Evidence of the first Paleo-Indians in the region dates back about 12,000 years. Yet it wasn't until the Late Woodland period (400–900 A.D.) that the park witnessed its earliest American Indian activity. While these people used primitive bows and arrows, they also built the Stone Fort on an 80-foot sandstone cliff near the park entrance.

Shelter caves used by American Indians have been documented within the park boundaries. There is one along Devil's Standtable Nature Trail where archeologists confirmed their presence from flint chips created while making spearheads and arrowheads. These remnants flake up from the soil's surface following rainfall. The other shelter cave is along the Indian Creek Shelter Trail. It is here scientists believe late Woodland Indians who stood no higher than 5 feet tall lived and worked. Smoke stains from their fires are still visible on the cave ceilings. Just below the bluff's drip line, flint and chert shards have been found as debris from the flint knapping process. Although no flint deposits exist in the park, one is nearby in Cobden, an 8-mile hike from the park.

It took numerous land purchases over the decades to amass the park's current acreage. Following the initial acquisition of the Rendleman farm, another 160 acres were acquired in 1946 in Jackson County, followed by 120 acres in 1963, some 110 acres in 1969, and 80 acres in 1970. Additional land buys were also made in Union County of 80 acres in 1961, some 830 acres in 1975, and 135 acres each in 1975 and 1979.

A research highlight was in an area now known as the Fern Rock Nature Preserve along the 2-mile Trillium Trail. During the late 1800s, two Illinois scientists—George Hazen French and Stephen A. Forbes—focused their botanical studies here, discovering rare plant species and habitats. Among their finds are French's Shooting Star, grove bluegrass, Forbes' saxifrage, and Synandra mint. It was first suggested that the park be named Fern Rock, but in recognition of the uniquely spectacular geology, Giant City won.

A campaign to preserve the area as a park started around 1900, but it wasn't until 1927 that the state government purchased 900 acres in Jackson and Union Counties from farmer Willis Rendleman. The park grew with additional land acquisitions ranging in size roughly from 100 to 200 acres. With most of the land bought from 1969 to 1975, the park today totals 4,055 acres. (Right, courtesy of Jackson County Historical Society.)

Willis Rendleman was the last private landowner of the main part of the park. His grandson, Allen Vancil of Makanda, recalls that his grandfather had read a newspaper article in early 1925 about the state government's program to buy land for state parks. (Both Allen Vancil.)

Rendleman hired a photographer to hike with him around his land, taking pictures of the geological features to send to Springfield. The state bought the land from Rendleman in 1927. (Both Allen Vancil.)

Since the park was established in 1927, nearly two dozen individual land purchases have been made over the years to account for its current 4,055 acres. (Both Allen Vancil.)

Farm families, including that of Allen Vancil, continued living "in the park" until the 1970s. Vancil grew up on a farm built by Willis Rendleman, which was surrounded by orchards where the Giant City Stables now stand off Giant City Road. He went to school at Rendleman School, which was off Giant City Road also. (Both Allen Vancil.)

As a boy growing up near the park, Allen Vancil crawled and climbed over all of the rocks and bluffs, often riding ponies to certain areas, and calls Giant City the "best playground." One landmark designating the county line between Jackson and Union Counties is Devil's Standtable. Here farmer Willis Rendleman leaped across the line to the "standtable" in Union County, while an unidentified fellow stands on the bluff in Jackson County. (Both Allen Vancil.)

The county line can be more easily found by the signs on Giant City Road, just south of the park's visitor center. It's important for park and lodge employees to know which county they are in if emergency services must be summoned. Retired park superintendent Bob Kristoff tended to consider the top of the bluff as Jackson County while the bottom was Union. (Both Allen Vancil.)

One legend of the park recounts secret meetings of the Knights of the Golden Circle, a band of secessionist civilians who organized as a secret society in the Union states of the Midwest, including Illinois, Indiana, and Ohio. Members in the Makanda-Cobden area abetted Union army deserters, who would hide among the area's hills. The park's caves were used for meetings. (Both Allen Vancil.)

Other families whose farms and orchards became park land include Agnew, Ashley, Deming, Kennedy, McGregor, Robert, and Vancil. (Both Allen Vancil.)

Makanda residents would seek shelter in the caves during storms. They also sought them out for relief from the humid summers. (Both Allen Vancil.)

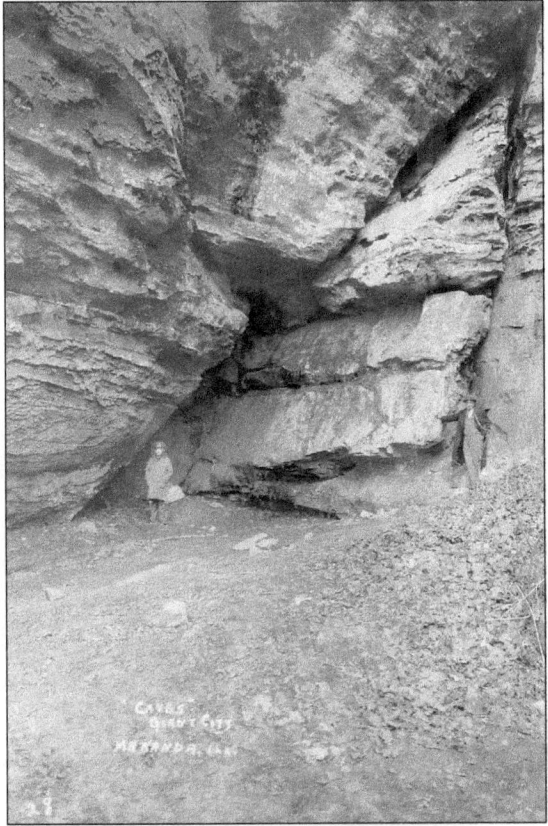

In the middle of the photograph below is the profile of an American Indian carved into the bluff face. As a young boy, Allen Vancil remembers visiting the carving when the headdress and face were intact. Over the years, the unprotected art has been defaced by vandals, though the head can still be seen. It can be found along the Trillium Trail. (Both Allen Vancil.)

The photograph above shows a famous spot for carving messages into the rock that has been used through the decades. At left is a group of hikers taking a break in the shadow of large rock formations. (Both Allen Vancil.)

As these photographs demonstrate, the park is well explored, and provides great opportunities for hiking and rock climbing. These images also highlight the park's geologic history. (Both Allen Vancil.)

Peach and apple orchards comprised much of the land. To help protect the crop, area orchardists asked the state to cut down all the red cedar trees in the park to prevent the spread of a tree fungus. Thankfully they said no. Willis Rendleman is pictured below. (Both Allen Vancil.)

# Two

# UNIVERSITY OF
# THE WOODS

Earl W. Dickey was already working hard when he enrolled in the Civilian Conservation Corps in 1934. One of 12 children, as a teenager he was swinging an axe to cut trees for coal mine props around Wayne City, Illinois. He was among 506,000 young men who joined ranks in one of the nation's largest work programs. The Civilian Conservation Corps' work from 1933 to 1941 resulted in the most dramatic man made developments at Giant City State Park. While Giant City Lodge is the crowning jewel of their work, these young men also built roads, bridges, trails, picnic shelters, and retaining walls, most of which still stand today as a testament to the quality of their planning, engineering, and execution.

When the CCC started, entry requirements allowed unmarried and unemployed men between the ages of 18 to 25 to enlist for six-month periods. The entry age dropped to 16 in 1935 at the peak of the Depression. They also were allowed to re-enlist. They each agreed to send home $22 to $25 of their $30 basic monthly allowance. In exchange, the men received three meals daily, lodging, clothing, basic medical and dental services, and as much vocational, recreational, or academic instruction as they wished.

CCC leadership was prepared to help transition the young men into camp life. "When a boy joins the CCC he comes into a life entirely new," *Stone-City Weekly* editors wrote. "He no longer has his family to look to for aid . . . He quickly learns the value of discipline. Cleanliness is stressed. Woodlore, the art of good fellowship, how to work with his hands, and to make the best of everything is impressed firmly upon his mind. No more valuable training for this great game of life is obtainable anywhere. A boy with a sheepskin from this great University of the Woods has something of which to be proud, a training that is unsurpassed."

"I do think the CCC helped prepare me for my life," Dickey recalled. "I worked all the way through college to help pay for my expenses. I did all kinds of repair jobs in the city and was a janitor at the college. I couldn't have done that without my CCC experience."

On Dickey's last day with the CCC, he helped fight a forest fire near Lake Superior. He went on to enroll at Adrian College in Michigan and then completed seminary school in New York. He was a Methodist minister for more than 50 years.

The men of Company #696 arrived in June 1933 at Giant City State Park, arriving by train in nearby Makanda following two weeks of basic training at Jefferson Barracks in St. Louis. They first lived in tents until the barracks pictured above were completed, just before winter set in. Men from Company #1657 arrived from Springfield in December 1933 to occupy a second camp, which was assigned to assist Company #696 until they left five months later in May 1934. The Company #692 men, including Earl W. Dickey, arrived at Camp Stone Fort in August 1934 until no more manpower was required to complete the park works and they were reassigned in November 1935 to Wisconsin. Company #696 was known as Camp Giant City. Its 200 men were assigned to Special Project 11, the lodge construction, from June 1933 to 1941. Company #1657 worked as Camp Stone Fort. Dickey said most of the men were able and steady workers since they were young. But some of them were young enough to never have been away from home. "You wouldn't believe how homesick some of those boys were. At night, they'd walk up and down the roads with tears just streaming down their faces. It was really hard on some of them," he said.

One of the main projects Earl W. Dickey worked on as a member of Camp Stone Fort was the construction of three septic tanks for the lodge. He is pictured above (middle) with Kenneth Bierbaum (left) of Marshall and George Mathias of Mount Olive as they were bending steel for the project. The Ford truck below is the same type he drove for work. One day Dickey was hauling gravel in one of the camp's oldest pick-up trucks when he pulled up at 3:55 p.m. for the last load and the front left wheel went flat. "The guys told me to just stay behind the wheel. A couple of them changed the tire while some others continued loading the gravel. In five minutes, I was on my way and I never left the truck. They really wanted to quit right at 4 o'clock," Dickey recalled. (Courtesy of Earl W. Dickey.)

While the men from the three camps were kept separate for most everything, they were allowed to spend time off together, including playing basketball. Teams from the camps across the southern Illinois region would play at nearby schools or churches. When the Giant City team won, Dickey remembers one of the captains treating the team to cake when they returned to camp. Playing a guard position, Dickey said his Giant City team captured the CCC state basketball championship in 1935 after cinching the title in a playoff game in Springfield. The men also played horseshoe games so competitive that double ringers were required to win, and dice, a game that often emptied some men's pockets of their monthly $5 allowance. They were also free to visit home on the weekends. Dickey occasionally worked for a Makanda storeowner who generously loaned him a pickup truck for a trip home. On one weekend visit, Dickey met his future wife, Juanita. (Left, Courtesy of R&M Kelley Corporation.)

The young men were advised to view the barracks as their homes, which were to be kept neat and orderly at all times. Each barracks had an assigned leader charged with policing cleanliness and discipline, and he would ask his men to perform duties as needed. Each man kept a trunk organized by his clothing record form. He'd be charged to replace any missing clothes or equipment, which could cost 18¢ for a summer undershirt, 90¢ for denim trousers, $2.15 for a comforter, or 59¢ for a canteen, for example. In all, the men were issued $85 worth of clothes and equipment by 1935 prices.

The men did practice exercise, not drills. The camp newspaper detailed an incident in which some of the locals were convinced the CCC men were preparing for military service. The article recounted how Captain Thorman, commanding officer of Company #696, "instituted retreat and we were given a few lessons in squad drills. We wish to take this opportunity to tell the public that we are not being trained for war but only learning to stand to attention, ease, and do a few drills, which are good exercises. Lieutenant Mathews was at Carbondale recently, and while there was asked by several if we were to receive guns before long, Lieutenant Mathews didn't scarcely know what his questioner meant until someone mentioned that the boys were drilled like soldiers. We are not, so do not believe all you hear. Rumors generally prove to be merely rumors."

MESS HALL CCC CO.D-691
CAMP STONE FORT MAKANDA. ILL.
CAPT. ER MORINE COMDR.

The men would rotate between various camp duties, including KP duty. Dickey recalled substituting KP duty with his colleagues who wanted off on weekends for 25¢. Each camp had its own mess hall, mess steward, and assigned seating with an assigned table leader. They were expected to remain standing until the steward ordered "Seats." Enrollees also were expected to follow the CCC's version of table manners. No "grabbing" was allowed, nor was profanity. Work clothes could be worn in the mess hall only for breakfast and dinner on workdays, and with special permission. (Courtesy of R&M Kelley Corporation.)

The federal government spent $3 million a year on food for all of its camps nationwide in 1935. Most of the food purchases were made locally, making a noticeable contribution to local economies. The food was generally considered plain, plentiful, and nutritious. Many of the enrollees had their first taste of "SOS" in the camps, which was typically served as creamed beef on toast. (Courtesy of R&M Kelley Corporation.)

Life in the camps revolved around the project work. Below, men are turning in their winter-issue clothes. In exchange, the summer dress included a cap, wool shirt, black tie, trousers, or breeches with leggings. The work wardrobe featured a fatigue hat, denim jumper or trousers, and service shoes. The photograph at right shows an outbuilding near the lodge work site. (Courtesy of R&M Kelley Corporation.)

Each camp prided itself on its available array of equipment and tools to get any job done. Supervisors would have to defend the need for additional equipment in detail within their lengthy requisition orders. The men worked 40-hour weeks with weekends off. Saturdays were used to make up lost time from bad weather. A lunch hour was included in the workday. This work time did not include camp duties or apply to those with leadership tasks. "Just as a workman puts in so many hours at his place of work and, when he returns home, has certain duties and chores to do around his home, so likewise, enrollees must perform such work," the enrollee handbook stated. (Courtesy of R&M Kelley Corporation.)

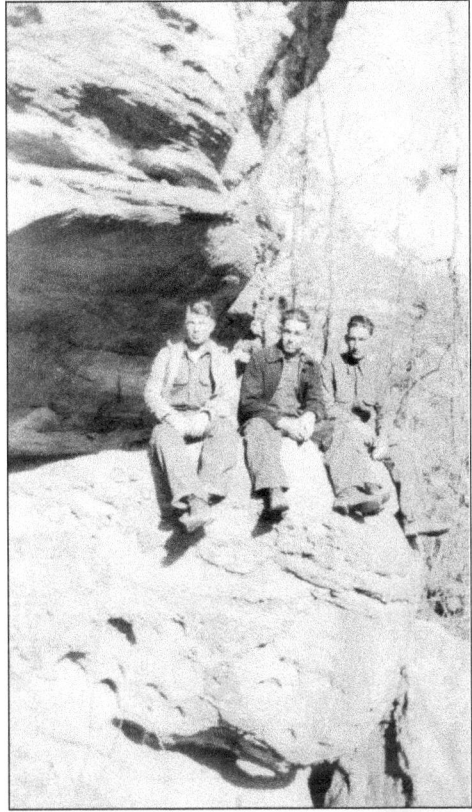

Some of the park's best tourists were the enrollees, who explored every ledge and bluff in the park. The men could buy chapbooks filled with small photographs of themselves posing in the park or at work sites to send home. The men were encouraged to use weekend passes to make visits home. They could leave following evening formation on Friday (if Saturday was not a work day) until 6:00 a.m. on Monday. Only a certain number of the enrollees were allowed off the camp at a time, and leave was only granted to each man once a month. (Right, courtesy of R&M Kelley Corporation.)

Earl Dickey spent 26 months with the CCC, first from August 1934 to November 1935 at Giant City State Park as a maintenance worker with Camp Stone Fort. His company, D-692, was then relocated to Mellen, Wisconsin, to work on Copper Falls State Park. He enrolled in the CCC because "you couldn't buy a job." Along with 506,000 men joining ranks with the CCC, Dickey was paid $30 a month, with $5 of it going into his pocket and the remaining $25 to his family in Wayne City in central Illinois. The camps allowed men aged 16 to 24. (Above, Courtesy of R&M Kelley Corporation.)

Girls, girls, girls . . . The camp newspaper included a column filled with good-natured innuendo, such as the cook who had six girls visiting from Dowell, why one fellow stopped going to Carterville every other night, who was called "Sweet Lips," who was the siren attracting Halley to Anna, and whether J. M. was hearing wedding bells or cow bells over the hills in Murphysboro. If the boys weren't with girls, they explored the region, including visiting the Du Quoin State Fair, took dance lessons, or read in the library. The library at Giant City was shared between the camps. It was converted "from what was considered a drab and uninteresting room," as detailed by the camp newspaper, into a room with freshly painted walls, tables, book racks, a new filing system, new lighting, smoking stands, and more magazines. (Courtesy of R&M Kelley Corporation.)

Arnel B. Adams 1st Lt Q.M. Res. Commanding
Harry J Mathews 2nd Lt. Sig. Res.
Hiram S. Jite 2nd Lt. Sig. Res.

Here are the boys of Camp Giant City, Company #696, CCC SP 11 in Makanda. The camp was in full operation from June 1933 to 1941. Segregation had not yet been outlawed, and the CCC had two camps for black men in Pomona and Alto Pass, although five black men are pictured among the Company #696 ranks. Commanding officers posed front and center of the photograph with

Roy R. Risk 1st Lt. Med. Res.
J. P. Britson, Camp Supt.
John M. Eddy, Ed. Adv.                    Photo Spencer & Wyckoff, Detroit.

the kitchen crew behind them in white. This photograph hangs in the lodge on the west wall of the original dining room on the way to the Bald Knob Room and under a light for easy viewing. (R&M Kelley Corporation.)

Motion pictures were shown monthly as a service by the National Park Service in Indianapolis. The first showings included screenings of *Daniel Boone*, *Cougar Hunt*, and *The Haunted Ship*, an animated feature.

The boys played plenty of sports, especially basketball and baseball. But they also enjoyed horseshoe pitching, boxing, softball, track, wrestling, and even soccer. They played teams from other camps, such as Mill Creek, Dowell, Pomona, Carterville, Sparta, and Mounds.

Easter Greetings

These are the covers from seasonal chap books ordered by the enrollees during their camp tours. The 3.5-inch-by-5-inch pocket albums held as many as eight 3-inch-by-3-inch photographs. These particular books belonged to Earl Schmidt and were published by The Baldwin Studio in St. Louis.

# Three

# SP 28C and More

Giant City Lodge stands on the park's highest ridge by design. CCC architects envisioned a structure blending naturally with its surroundings. The National Park Service at the time described the park as "rolling to rugged hill country, an extension of the Ozark Mountains. Stone formations of exceptional scenic interest are numerous. Some of the most interesting stone formations occur where huge blocks of rock have separated and shifted to form precipitous cliffs with passages between that resemble city streets. Overgrown now with trees, grass, ferns, and other plants, the scene suggests a long abandoned ruin of a city of antiquity. In this setting, a fine stone lodge built of native stone and timber could provide a lounge, public toilets, and dining room service."

The lodge was known to the CCC as Project 28C, and it was often referred to as the "lodge house" in various documents. Its layout was perfected as construction progressed. For example, the floor was originally planned for concrete and then a maple wood floor was discovered to be less expensive. In the end, hand-hewn white oak planks were used. The second-level balcony was first designed to wrap around the entire lobby on all four sides, but was altered on the south end to accommodate the soaring two-story fireplace. And though a basement did not appear in the first blueprints, one was added as construction progressed.

Although a National Park Service inspector would make much ballyhoo during the lodge's early years for allowing dancing, CCC architects intended the lobby to host dancing all along. Inspector Arnold Kruger must be rolling in his grave to know that there is still dancing during special occasions in the 21st century.

When the time neared to transfer lodge ownership from the federal to state government, an idea to name it after the Alamo in Texas was proposed. Yet it was one of the assistant architects, Joseph Golabowski, who insisted on Giant City Lodge to fit the character of the structure and the surroundings from which it was built.

Over the years, the dining room and kitchen have been added on to or renovated to accommodate more diners, but the only other major project extensively altering the lodge was completed in 1987 under the Build Illinois program, a statewide public works and infrastructure improvement program. This project doubled the lodge's dining capacity, added banquet space, and built 24 more cabins.

Work by Company #696 on the lodge started in June 1934. As work progressed, it was evident more men were needed, and Company #692 was called in and worked on the project from August 1934 until November 1935. This put nearly 400 men to work.

While the CCC work program was intended to teach trades, create jobs, and build public works, the men working on the lodge as carpenters, stone masons, and in other skilled craftsman positions learned their job skills so well that their work rivaled that of local professionals.

Project 28C is what the CCC called the lodge when work officially started in June 1934 by Company #696. Corps architects wanted to show off the area's natural beauty, factoring the location and future tree growth into the site and design of the lodge. The original lodge construction was built in three units: a refectory (dining area), the comfort station (restrooms), and the central unit housing the main lobby. (Courtesy of R&M Kelley Corporation.)

It took CCC work crews a little more than two years to build the lodge, beginning in June 1934 and finishing in time for an August 1936 dedication. Men from Companies #696 and #692 toiled together on a variety of tasks: quarrying stone, blacksmithing, hewing timber, carpentry, building roads and trails, driving trucks, cooking meals, or office clerking. (Courtesy of R&M Kelley Corporation.)

Designed by CCC engineers, the lodge featured three main units: a refectory (the dining area), the comfort station with its restrooms, and the lounge (the central lobby area). The lobby included a two-story fireplace and a wraparound balcony. Toward the end of construction, several people wanted to name it after the Alamo because of its similar rustic appearance. Yet it was a National Park Service assistant architect who insisted the building stand on its own unique features and enjoy its own identity as Giant City Lodge.

Although the federal government alone paid the $650,000 to plan and build the lodge and its initial six cabins, it was critical to the CCC leadership that Illinois government officials understand their new long-term responsibility to maintain and care for the lodge. (Courtesy of R&M Kelley Corporation.)

Much of the wood used in the lodge's construction was hewn on site. The beams, pillars, doors, main lobby, and balcony floors and lintels are all white oak. The building was originally built with hand-split oak shingles, which have long since been replaced with modern roofing. For maximum durability, pecan wood was ordered from nearby lumberyards (such as Egyptian Lumber Company in Cobden) for the circular stairways to the balcony. (R&M Kelley Corporation.)

William Bodeker of Murphysboro, a member of Company #696, was one of six or seven stonecutters whose task was to cut and face the sandstone used in the lodge construction. He said the stone came from the northwest part of the park. A big air compressor was set on the hill, with hose stretching out 200 feet to reach the stonecutters.

Robert Kingery, Illinois Department of Public Works and Buildings director, stated the federal government's intentions in a Dec. 1, 1934, letter: "When the building of Giant City is completed, it is our intention to operate it by state employees direct or by entering into a contract with someone to operate it for the state. I rather lean toward the latter because it gives assurance of continuity of management that is not certain under direct political appointment or civil service." The lodge's restaurant and cabin services have been continuously contracted to concessionaires from 1934 to today. A World War I Liberty truck was used to set the 30- to 40-foot tall white oak pillars upright; they extend from the basement floor to the ceiling of the central lounge. (Courtesy of R&M Kelley Corporation.)

Built from local sandstone, the lodge's stone masonry was completed by CCC crews who were trained on site. Their work cutting and setting the stone is so precise that it is said the work rivaled local professional masons. The stones are held together with a 1 to 4 mixture of mortar, except in the archways where 10 percent more cement was used. Roughly 15 bags of cement were used per 100 cubic feet. (Courtesy of R&M Kelley Corporation.)

Landscaping was focused on sidewalks, curbing, and a stairway leading to the lodge front door. Trees native to the region were selected for the plantings. (Courtesy of R&M Kelley Corporation.)

Final work projects to complete the lodge were the responsibility of the state. The federal emergency conservation work fund did not allow for purchase of heating, lighting, plumbing, furniture, and kitchen equipment. The $11,000 needed to equip the lodge with these items symbolized the federal government's passing of the buck to state officials. (Courtesy of R&M Kelley Corporation.)

From July 21 to August 25, 1935, the CCC recorded 4,317 visitors on Sundays only, with 436 of them from out of state and "practically represent[ing] a roll call of every state in the Union," according to the *Stone-City Weekly* newspaper. "Every Sunday an almost unbroken line of cars streams into the park. One sees every type and vintage of automobile represented, from a 1916 Model T Ford to a 1935 custom-built model. The richest and the humblest intermingle as visitors and picnickers."

A formal handoff of the lodge between governments happened at a dedication ceremony on August 30, 1936, led by Gov. Henry Horner. As many as 20,000 people are believed to have attended. (Courtesy of R&M Kelley Corporation.)

CCC architects sited the lodge on the park's highest ridge. The idea was to offer visitors a spectacular vista of the surrounding hills. The view at the time ranged up to 10 miles.

These two images contrast some subtle changes in the lodge from the 1950s to the 1960s. Besides the maturation of the vegetation, the neon sign appearing in the top image was gone by the 1960s. A National Park Service inspector in a May 1938 report noted the "gaudy neon sign" and recommended it be taken down at that time. (Courtesy of R&M Kelley Corporation.)

That May 1938 report did force some immediate changes at the lodge. "The disquieting element in Giant City State Park is the operation of the lodge," inspector Arnold Kugler reported. The "spectacular display of gaudy neon advertising signs" on the front of the lodge and around the railings were ordered out when Kugler claimed they reminded him of a "hot-dog stand at Coney Island." "Cheap tables and chairs" interspersed with the good ones were replaced. The lack of appropriate furniture, according to Kugler, "is an incentive to the nefarious behavior of the night-time visitors." A Victrola played dance music. He also noticed that beer was sold during church hours on Sunday morning. "This 'Babel' cannot persist if we expect to retain the favor of public opinion in the operation of our State Parks," the inspector said in the report, adding that the nighttime activity may have been promoted by the park's recreational counselor at the time.

Any changes to the lodge were minor compared to the 1987 addition. Before that, the original Bald Knob room was added in 1985 and the Shawnee dining room was opened in 1969. The Shawnee room memorializes the Shawnee American Indians who crossed the region on the Trail of Tears while the Bald Knob room honors the giant cross in Alto Pass, visible from the park.

This photograph shows some of the early changes to the main lounge. In the back of the room is a bar to the left, which was originally designed as a concession stand. To the right is the conversion of what was originally planned as a museum-quality exhibit area into a gift shop. Today the gift shop's glass counter in the foreground is where a preserved adult buffalo and calf are on permanent display from Bison Bluff Farms in Cobden, whose bison meat is featured on the lodge's menu.

Now called the lobby, the lodge's lounge was originally outfitted with hand-built white oak furniture and American Indian accessories. Again, it was the ably trained CCC work crews who built the oak furniture. When they rolled back the rugs at the Giant City State Park lodge for a dance, they rolled up about $3,000 worth of handmade Indian rugs. These, along with pottery and baskets, were bought from the Navajo tribe of Oklahoma. Concessionaire Anna Cook commented in a 1945 newspaper article that government employees traveled to Oklahoma to ensure the purchases were authentic. All of the items have disappeared over the years.

The menu's tradition of fried chicken dinners started when the lodge opened in August 1938. A menu from April 1938 featured a $1 fried chicken dinner with a choice of tomato juice, shrimp cocktail, or fruit cocktail; congealed vegetable salad, lettuce salad, or sliced tomatoes; new potatoes, whole French-fried carrots, or green beans; imported cheeses, chocolate sundae, or apple pie with snappy cheese. The original dining room is where the hostess stand and lounge area are now located. Today's version of the fried chicken dinner is similar, but is served as an all-you-can-eat, family-style meal served at the table and features homemade dumplings, mashed potatoes, country gravy, green beans, corn, cole slaw, and biscuits.

The lodge plans originally featured six guest cabins and a separate shower house, but an additional six were built in 1937. State officials had requisitioned another 12 cabins—double cabins with bath facilities—in June 1942, but never received approval because of the war. The double cabin concept, however, would resurface in the 1987 construction of the Prairie cabins. By 1946, the existing 12 cabins were modernized with the addition of plumbing and electricity; the cabin walls were plastered over at this time as well.

The cost to rent a cabin in 1941 was $4 a night. They did not include bathrooms. Instead, visitors had to share a shower house. Known as the Historic cabins immediately south of the lodge, they have been rebuilt or remodeled three times over the years.

The Historic cabins today are outfitted and decorated in much the same manner as the original cabins, if not simpler. They all have two full beds as opposed to twin beds, comforters instead of chenille bedspreads, blinds instead of curtains, and a television instead of a radio. Perhaps the biggest difference is the addition of plumbing, heat, and air conditioning.

Lodge records show that a new dishwasher and new back bar for souvenirs was installed in 1953. Among that work was the addition of even more neon signs, claimed to help promote more sales at the lodge.

Until 1987, concessionaires at the lodge had been paying sales tax to the wrong county. It turns out they were paying Jackson County its sales tax. However, when a $6 million renovation of the lodge opened the door for year-round business at the lodge, one Union County government official started thinking about how much more his county would see in additional revenue. But some checking revealed that the tax checks had been cut to Jackson County. It turned out the county line runs near the ball diamond on Youth Camp Road, just north of the lodge.

The water tower with the observation platform located on the lodge site was built in 1971 to supply the entire park with water. The tank was built by Universal Tank and Iron Works, Inc. of Indianapolis. The tank stands 82 feet high and holds 100,000 gallons of water. The tower has an observation platform that is 50 feet above ground, providing a majestic view of the surrounding countryside, including the 111-foot-high cross on Bald Knob Mountain at nearby Alto Pass. In 1972 the Illinois Department of Conservation won the "Steel Tank of the Year" award in the elevated tank category from the Steel Plate Fabricators Association.

This photograph taken in 1954 depicts the back side of the lodge and also captures the rate of tree maturation around the property. The road leading to the back door has been replaced with sidewalks, the CCC worker statue, a flagpole, and a circular drive winding past the Historic cabins. The trees have since topped the sightline from the lodge balcony, infringing on any clear view of the hillsides. The construction of a new water tower featuring an observation platform in 1971 restored this dramatic viewing opportunity for visitors.

The CCC's handiwork on the stone retaining walls along Giant City Creek has withstood the decades. However, the original sheltered benches and the original bridges have been replaced over the years, mostly for safety reasons. (Courtesy of R&M Kelley Corporation.)

Earl Dickey's first job at Giant City was on a road-building crew, working first on the road between the men's barracks in the lodge parking lot to the park's main road, now called Giant City Lodge Road. The men ended up building nearly 24 miles of road, removing trees and stumps, grading the roadbed, and transporting surface materials. CCC roads were distinctive because of the timber guardrails or stacked stone retaining walls used as curbing. Dickey pointed out that there's no cement holding the stones in the retaining walls along the roadways; only the walls along the creek banks have cement to withstand water. (Courtesy of R&M Kelley Corporation.)

Perhaps ironically, CCC crews had to blast their way through the same rock layers that produced the park's unique features to complete the road and bridge building. (Courtesy of R&M Kelley Corporation.)

Trail markers originally blazed the way for visitors along the park roads to interesting spots throughout the park. Made by the hewing department, the markers were made of carved and painted wood and were used to point the way to the shelter houses and parking lots. (Courtesy of R&M Kelley Corporation.)

VIEW FROM NORTH CLIFF
NEAR NORTH ENTR

DITCHING
GANG
#27

Woodworking and landscaping were among the trades learned by corpsmen. The Giant City men earned a reputation for training master craftsmen, allowing them to ply their skills in the trades after their time with the CCC.

While the bridge spans lasted until the 1980s, most of the bridge abutments are still functional. Two had to be replaced when numerous trees fell during a rare type of inland hurricane called a *derecho* and crushed the stonework in 2009. (Courtesy of R&M Kelley Corporation.)

Even as the men were released from CCC duties, the federal government followed their employment. When Joseph A. Bangiolo, a Camp Stone Fort foreman, was released from the camp on November 3, 1935, his papers noted he had a "secure position" with the Work Progress Administration.

Visitors travel over these bridges today. The top bridge is near the intersection of Church Road and Giant City Lodge Road at the park's service center. The other crosses Giant City Creek near Shelter Five.

Salvaging Gravel

#6

Earl Dickey's work at the park was first with a road gang. The work would stop for an hour lunch. Dickey would volunteer to stay with the tools, giving him extra time to hone his skills with a hatchet and an opportunity to earn a chance to get off early for the day.

Work on the roads was tedious. The roadbed had to be raised, hand graded, and then topped with gravel. Side channels paralleling the road carried away water runoff. (Courtesy of R&M Kelley Corporation.)

It was common to see men climbing up trees in search of the ideal limb for wooden pieces. Besides having to elevate themselves, they would have to just as carefully bring up their tools and then haul down the useable limbs. (Courtesy of R&M Kelley Corporation.)

No renovations or major additions took place at the lodge after 1945, when the kitchen and dining room space was added to accommodate 100 guests. In 1985, the state broke ground on a $5 million upgrade project that included a dining room and banquet room addition, more kitchen space, and 22 new cabins on the north and west sides of the lodge complex.

The renovation work included reconfiguring the front and back lodge entrances to improve handicapped accessibility. An asphalt sidewalk from the main parking lot and a ramp near the front door were added. A circular driveway with a level sidewalk leading directly into the new Bald Knob dining room was added as well. In the middle of the circle driveway stands the CCC Worker statue, which was dedicated in 2006.

This aerial view shows the footprints of the Prairie cabins, which are basically a duplex offering an adjoining door between the two individual units. The duplex idea was originally proposed as a later phase when the Historic cabins were designed, but the war interfered. The new construction again allowed accommodation for handicapped access. A housekeeping building and pool house were also built at the time.

The expanded Bald Knob Room was the third dining addition to the lodge. The first one was in 1941 when a dining porch and an expanded kitchen area were added. The second renovation in 1948 was when the Shawnee Room was enclosed for additional dining space and the original Bald Knob Room was added as a room parallel to the main dining room. The 1987 addition doubled capacity in the main dining room and added convertible banquet space for family gatherings, special occasions, and meetings.

The $5 million renovation of the lodge included the construction of a new dining room, handicapped accessible entrances, storage facilities, and heating and cooling systems. Once completed in 1987, the new dining room area offered the addition of an adjustable banquet room. A game room, hot tub, and sauna were part of the new basement space, but were closed within a couple of years.

The lodge addition was possible thanks to the Build Illinois state grant program under Gov. James Thompson's administration. Helping fund the grant program was a soda pop tax designated specifically for Build Illinois projects. To celebrate the occasion and celebrate a CCC anniversary, CCC men were invited to the festivities and are pictured here with Governor Thompson.

# Four

# Around the Park

Giant City has had more than one kind of copperhead hiding among the bluffs. While the venomous snakes tend to avoid human contact, so did Confederate sympathizers known as Copperheads for their clandestine commiserating during the Civil War—at least that is what history suggests. Legend has it that men who supported the Confederate cause would meet under cloak of darkness in the remote woods of the park, because the region generally followed Illinois' official position as a Union state.

After the war, scientists with Southern Illinois Normal University (SINU) also took to the woods and would wander the unique habitat called Fern Rock Natural Area, a 170-acre area along the Trillium Trail near the park's main entrance. The importance of this portion of the Shawnee Hills as a natural science study area was recognized as early as 1870 when SINU botanist George Hazen French named the area for its abundance of ferns, including Christmas, marginal, maidenhair, lady, and several spleenwort fern species.

The forested portions of Fern Rock are dominated by oaks and hickories or by maples. Outstanding sandstone cliffs, bluffs, and shelter communities support a large variety of vegetation. Along the north-facing slope, shade-loving species are found, including mosses and liverworts. Notable crevice-occurring species are Forbes' saxifrage, partridgeberry, and small alumroot. Fern Rock is where French discovered two plants in the late 1800s—French's shooting star and Forbes' saxifrage. The area contains one of the most spectacular spring wildflower displays to be seen anywhere in the state, and was designated as a state nature preserve in August 1973.

Also earning historical titles and places on the National Register of Historic Places are the Stone Fort site on August 2, 2002, and the lodge and cabins on March 4, 1985. The men who comprised the CCC workforce received their homage in 2002, when a bronze statute depicting a worker was installed behind the lodge.

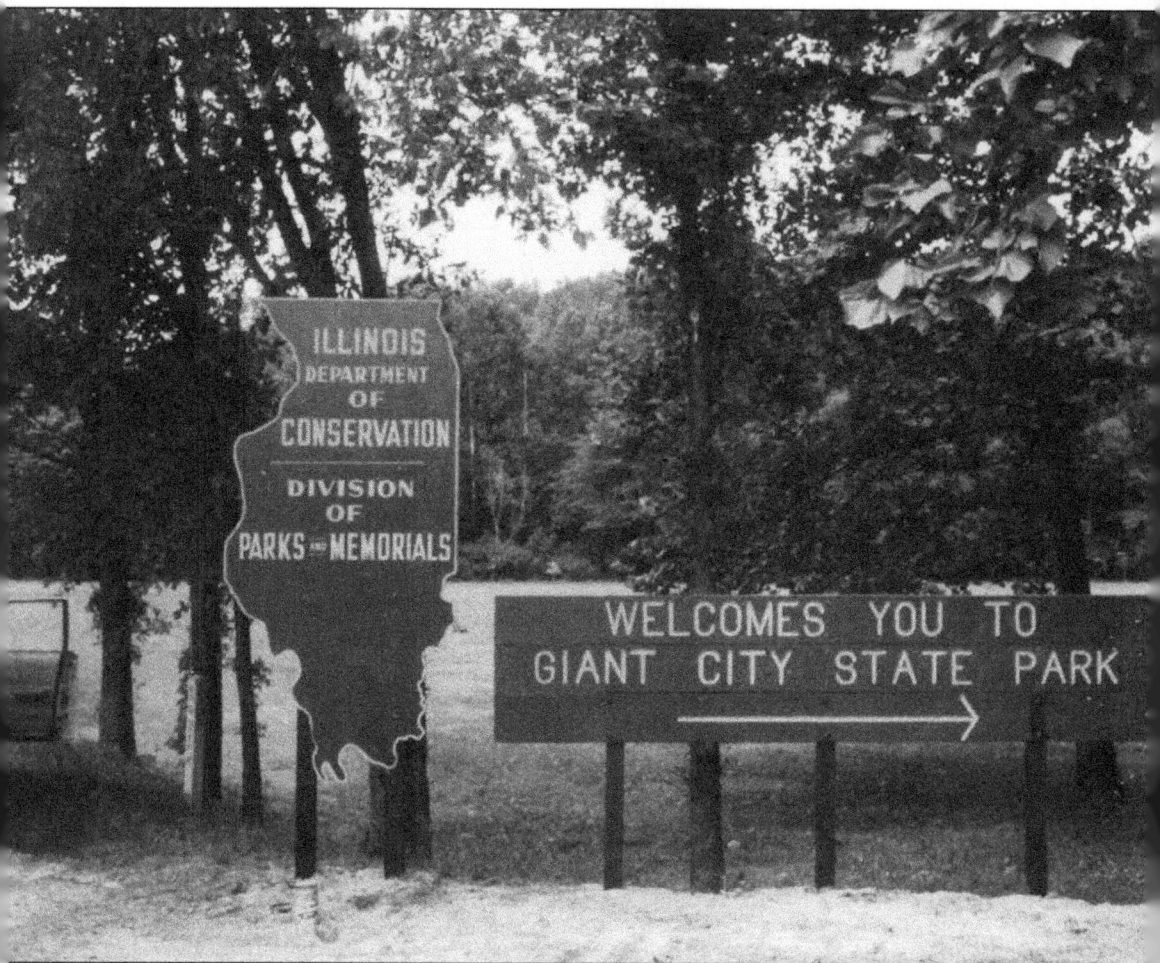

Giant City has always been a state park, but there have been a variety of entities overseeing its operation. During the lodge construction, it was under the administration of the Illinois Department of Public Works and Buildings. It was then run by the Illinois Department of Conservation, and is now overseen by the Illinois Department of Natural Resources.

It was estimated that upwards of 20,000 people a year were visiting Giant City before it was officially designated as a park. One of the subjects in the Farmer photograph above rode in on horseback. (Courtesy of Jackson County Historical Society.)

FARMER PHOTO

SCENE NEAR MAKANDA, ILL.

People visiting Giant City before it was an official park would travel into the area on dirt roads cleared by farmers with adjacent fields or orchards. In the late 1920s, shortly after the park was established, area farmers complained regularly about access roads being gated off from their use. (Courtesy of Jackson County Historical Society.)

This is an outing of an unidentified church congregation and Sunday school. Notice the barefoot boy and all of the litter. The park and lodge remain a popular destination for families after church. (Courtesy of Jackson County Historical Society.)

People flocked to Giant City State Park to enjoy its wooded setting as soon as the early 1800s. While the state bought the land comprising the heart of the park in 1927, the picnic shelter and comfort station featured in this 1935 photograph were built by CCC work crews. Each shelter features a double fireplace, built-in benches, and plenty of room for picnic tables. This group likely crossed the bridge below to reach Shelter Two.

Giant City has always been a popular field trip destination for schools, whether to teach earth science, biology, or botany, for a guided hike, or to make maple syrup.

This couple was a popular subject during a public relations shoot in the late 1940s.

Here is the happy couple again, this time snapping a photograph of their own in front of the lodge and enjoying the vista. Allegedly the perch allowed a view of the surrounding 10 miles.

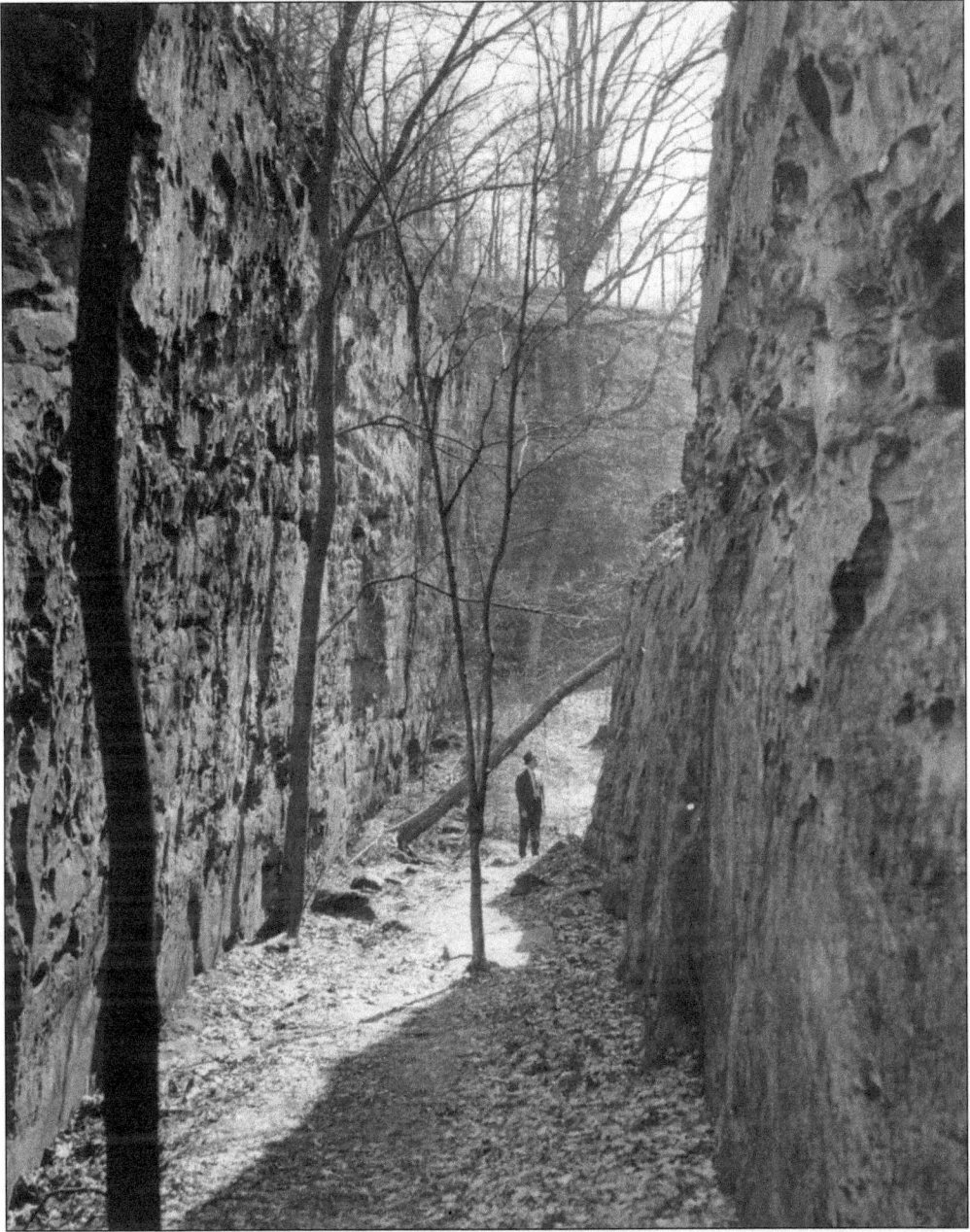

The CCC was created under Pres. Franklin D. Roosevelt's Works Progress Administration. The CCC was also known as the Emergency Conservation Work program.

Construction of new campsites took place in the 1970s.

Trips to the park tend to center around food, whether a picnic or a fried chicken dinner at the lodge. The park shelters offered a choice of fireplaces or fire rings near the shelters for cooking. (Courtesy of Jackson County Historical Society.)

The group in the top picture is in the original dining room, complete with a photograph of Illinois Gov. Dwight H. Green (1941–1949) on the fireplace mantle. Today this area hosts the bar, lounge, and the hostess station. The kids below romp in the lodge lobby. It is likely that the rugs in the foreground are the original American Indian versions. (Courtesy of R&M Kelley Corporation.)

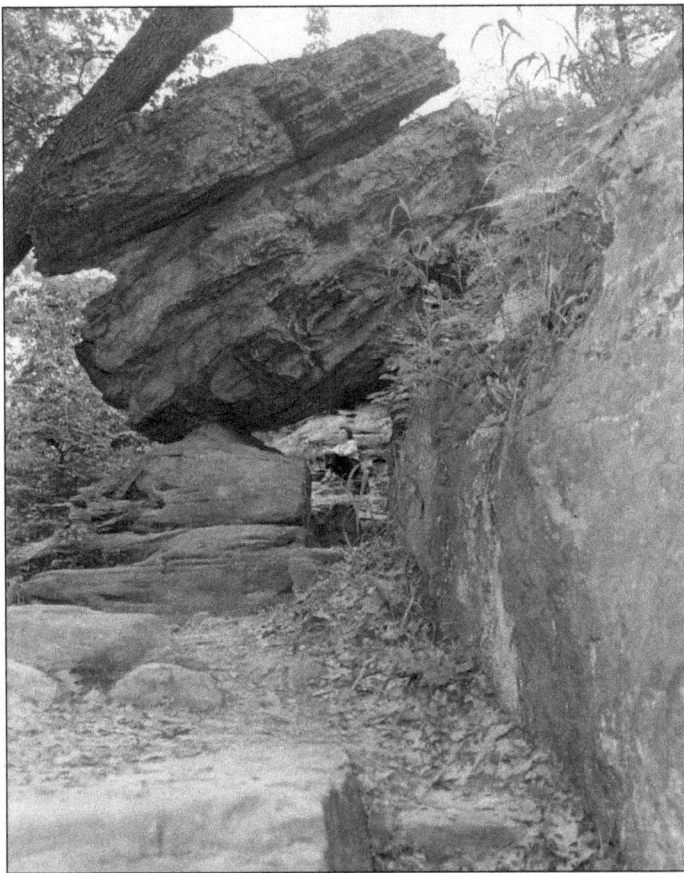

Another shoot in the public relations series finds a young woman during a reflective moment. Below, some senior citizens are gathered in the lodge lobby for a presentation. There is a giant projector near the speaker, and the jukebox stands ready toward the back of the group. (Courtesy of Jackson County Historical Society.)

One of the most prominent of the 31 kinds of wildlife roaming the park is the whitetail deer. In the 1960s the park had maintained what was known as the "deer pen" near the visitor center, granting visitors an up-close look at the official state mammal. Other flora and fauna include 30 varieties of ferns, 201 kinds of birds, more than 50 types of reptiles and amphibians, and more than 900 flowering plants, including more than 80 tree species. Other state symbols—the white oak (state tree), the blue violet (state flower), the bluegill (state fish), and the cardinal (state bird)—live within the park. A variety of plant and animal endangered species are protected within the park's boundaries, including the Synandra mint, which can be found in the Fern Rocks Natural Area, and the golden mouse. Wild turkeys were once endangered, but they have proliferated enough to allow for a hunting season.

Rappelling and rock climbing are common sports in the park, often attracting ROTC classes, outdoors clubs, and Scouts to the bluffs. Rangers have had more trouble with casual visitors who attempt to jump on Devil's Standtable or get stuck in Fat Man's Squeeze, which is no longer an official feature on the Giant City Nature Trail.

Besides recreational rappelling, numerous emergency rescue teams practice at the park, including the Little Egypt Search and Rescue Team, which conducted many of its exercises on the bluffs near Shelter Two.

"Behind Giant City Park beauty is a chance for death or injury" was the headline in a September 1979 Associated Press article about a trend of alcohol-related injuries. There were two accidents in 1975 and 1979 that resulted in four deaths. A report indicated 20 bluff accidents, 21 traffic accidents, and 21 personal injury accidents. Two of the fatalities were from bluff falls, and two were from traffic collisions. In both traffic accidents, the operators of motorcycles were killed. Most of the personal injury accidents were minor cuts and bruises or insect stings. But 11 of the 20 bluff falls resulted in serious injuries. SIU students were involved in 11 of the more serious injury cases, and more than three-fourths of the cases involved alcohol. Alcohol is banned from the park during the SIU fall and spring semesters.

Giant City has always been a family-oriented destination. Beyond the hikes, picnics, camping, and lodge dinners, the park also offers fishing, hunting, horseback riding, morel (mushroom) hunting, bird watching, and more.

# Five

# INTRODUCING THE HOSTS

At the center of the lodge have been the concessionaires, who offer bids to the state to win the contracts to provide lodging and dining services.

The folks who have run the lodge since its opening in 1938 are Clairent Hopkins of Marion, Anna Cook of Royalton, George Whitney of Carrier Mills, Mary Vaughn of Zeigler, Clarence Palmier of Carbondale, James Depper of Alton, and Richard and Mike Kelley of Carbondale. The father-son team of Richard and Mike Kelley celebrate 30 years of operation during the 2010 season, and they surpassed 1.5 million people served in 2008.

"The first two years were long and fun. It's the getting there that's so much fun," Mike Kelley said, adding that he was only 19 years old when they took over the business. At the time, the dining room capacity was 100 people between the original dining room, the Shawnee Room, and the original Bald Knob Room. Some locals might recall the old wagon wheel lights, green floor tile, screened windows, and the drapery.

The Kelleys keep these memories in two scrapbooks so big that Richard straps them closed with forgotten belts left behind by cabin guests. The pages are crammed with menus, licenses, photographs, thank-you letters, letters of complaint, school group drawings, and even pressed flower corsages that they used to give to the servers who were mothers working on Mother's Day.

Since it's a family business, the pictures include wedding day pictures for Mike and his sister Kathy (both weddings held in the off-season so as not to interfere with the lodge business) and dozens of birthdays, anniversaries, and other special occasions. Richard also is responsible for maintaining business ledgers charting how many diners were served, the day's dining revenues, cabin occupancy, and weather conditions every day. A row of red ledgers sits neatly on a shelf behind his desk in the original Bald Knob Room. Those ledgers show that they served 49,441 people in 1981, a number that grew to 126,121 in 2009.

Richard's collection of autographed political figures attracts attention and occasional snide comments. On the wall by the lodge office, he has displayed pictures of presidents, governors, state officers, local assemblymen, and others. Arkansas governor Bill Clinton loved the lodge's chicken, which he enjoyed while running for president.

Park custodian Jack Perschbacher shares a quiet moment at the lodge (above). He was likely the one who designed and presented the float (below) in the 1959 Apple Festival Parade in Murphysboro.

Richard and Mike Kelley took over the lodge concession in 1981. They received notice from the state only 30 days before it was scheduled to open for the season. That year, they launched what would become an annual tradition of the staff dressing up for Halloween. Like most southern Illinoisans, the Kelleys are avid Cardinals fans. Notice the bar behind Mike. The original bar was in the lobby where the lodge office is now. (Courtesy of R&M Kelley Corporation.)

With crowds swelling up to 1,600 people on Mother's Day and Easter, the lodge keeps a stable of servers on hand, roughly half of them SIU students working their way through school. The girls dressed in white were table bussers. Over the years their uniforms adopted a unisex look, and more men now work in the dining room. The lodge has employed about 50 part-time positions, including office staff, housekeepers, servers, bussers, dishwashers, and cooks. (Courtesy of R&M Kelley Corporation.)

Richard and Mike Kelley pose in the newly opened Bald Knob Room in the 1987 dining room addition, which also included a convertible banquet space. They worked two years with park, state conservation, and other officials to complete the project. The new banquet space did include another fireplace, but it did not work properly, and a wall was built over it. (Courtesy of R&M Kelley Corporation.)

A frequent visitor to the lodge continues to be Gov. James Thompson and his family, pictured here in 1981 with the Kelley family. The governor discovered the lodge by chance after some staffers suggested he visit for a meal. Richard collects autographed photographs from politicians who visit the lodge and displays them on a wall in the lodge office. The image below with the late U.S. senator Paul Simon was taken in 1982 during the wedding reception of Simon's daughter, Sheila, at the lodge. (Courtesy of R&M Kelley Corporation.)

# The Lodge

## GIANT CITY STATE PARK
### MAKANDA, ILLINOIS
Phone 2F14   Carbondale, Ill.

Numerous species
of moths and butter
flies are obtain-
able in the park
at this time.

Our Today's

Special Family Style
Dinner menu

includes
the following

$1.00 plus tax

WELCOME

SPECIAL

Order Ham Salad
Saratoga Flakes
Sliced Tomato
Bread, butter
and drink.

$ .50

Entree
Country Style fried Chicken, Country Club fried or baked ham
or Steak

. Vegatables

New Potatoes
Buttered Peas

Pickle Beet

Bread and Butter

Salads

Desserts
Fresh Rhubarb Pie
Neopolatian Jello
Raspberry Sherbert
Chocolate Sundae

Shredded Cabbage
Navy Beans

Combination

Iced Tea, Coffee or
Milk

---

**SPECIAL**

Plate of Cold Cuts, Potato Salad, Bread and Butter
Choice of Desserts and Drink
SEVENTY-FIVE CENTS

---

Steak or Fried Chicken
Sandwich with Potatoes
and "End Salad"
FIFTY CENTS

Cold Cut Country Club Baked Ham
or Beef with Potato Salad, Bread
and Butter and Drink
SIXTY CENTS

---

**A LA CARTE**

| | | | |
|---|---|---|---|
| T-Bone Steak | $1.00 | ½ Fried Chicken | $1.00 |
| Sirloin Steak | 1.00 | ¼ Fried Chicken | .65 |
| Club or Rib Steak | .75 | Fried Chicken, country style cut up for 2 | 2.00 |

---

This is a copy of a souvenir menu from 1941. The reference to Saratoga Flakes is an old-fashioned term for Saltines, which was a name devised by the U.S. Army for the crackers included in mess rations. The lodge continues to serve the fried chicken dinner today.

# Six

# MAKANDA

Sitting as the northern entrance to Giant City State Park, the scenic village of Makanda was once a thriving fruit-shipping locale that today is home to a unique bedroom community of artists and craftsmen. It also reigns supreme as the host of the unique Vulture Fest in the fall, an annual gathering of folks who love music, art, and especially gazing at the hundreds of turkey vultures that take roost in the surrounding canyon every year.

Located about 8 miles south of Carbondale and about 43 miles north of the state's southernmost point where the Mississippi and Ohio Rivers converge, the village wasn't incorporated until 1888. By that time, though, it already was a busy shipping point for juicy peaches and apples, among other fruits, that growers soon realized would thrive in near-perfect growing conditions. Peaches, for instance, are rarely stung by late spring frosts, in part because of the region's topography and altitude.

The Illinois Central Railroad laid its tracks right through Makanda, and the depot finished in 1857. Just four years later the first 4,000 peach trees bore their first marketable fruit crop. But the northern gateway to Giant City State Park turned sleepier once the region's fruit principals decided to move the main shipping center to nearby Cobden in the early 1900s. Today the village, which covers 4.3 square miles and has a population of about 400, boasts a unique collection of artists and craftsmen selling their wares out of some storefronts that were part of the original Makanda boardwalk in the late 1850s. Makanda has about 180 households and 29 businesses, according to 2007 Census Bureau data. Perhaps its most famous resident of all time is former U.S. Sen. Paul Simon, a 1988 presidential candidate.

This idyllic drawing of Makanda was done in the 1850s, just as the railroad had come through the valley. In the latter part of the 1800s, the regionally popular M. M. Thompson's Hotel (No. 9) sat just across from the start of Makanda's present day "boardwalk." The former Rendleman and Thompson General Merchants building on the corner still stands today. The village's depot (No. 13) no longer exists, and the space is now used for parking for boardwalk businesses and community events. (Courtesy of Jackson County Historical Society.)

The village's Methodist church had a total of 25 members as of the fall of 1877. Three other churches within Makanda Township brought the total number of Methodist members to 140, according to an account by W. F. Hopkins. (Courtesy of Jackson County Historical Society.)

This photograph shows the Makanda boardwalk at the town's peak. The L. L. Bell name painted on the building façade has been maintained over the years. Shopkeepers today include the Makanda Trading Company, Rainmaker Art Studio, Visions Gallery, and Southern Sisters Workshop. (Courtesy of Jackson County Historical Society.)

A customer walks up to the R. E. Bridges general store in the late 1800s. The building used to sit at the corner of Main Street and Baptist Church Road. (Courtesy of Jackson County Historical Society.)

Downtown Makanda during the mid-1800s shows a busy boardwalk with Sumner's Supply hardware store, a barbershop, and a druggist. The L. L. Bell name can be seen on the front of the middle building. The residence on top of the hill and visible just over the boardwalk roofline belonged to Dr. Thomas Agnew.

The Makanda depot, completed in 1857, quickly became the hub of the community as the Makanda area grew into one of Illinois' busiest fruit growing and shipping locales. The area wasn't platted until 1863, and it wasn't incorporated until 1888, well after Makanda Township was established in 1874. (Courtesy of Jackson County Historical Society.)

An Illinois Central Railroad spotter runs the rails over the Drury Creek Bridge in 1894. By that time, some 40 years since the ICRR set up shop throughout the Drury Creek Valley, Makanda was a bustling, business-rich community with a mere 100 residents. (Courtesy of Jackson County Historical Society.)

The photograph above shows a part of Church Street near downtown in the late 1880s. The image below shows Church Street looking north in the late 1800s. Some believe the village of Makanda got its name from a longtime Kaskaskia Indian chief named Kanda, but that origin has never been verified. (Courtesy of Jackson County Historical Society.)

During the early 1900s, downtown Makanda continued as a hub of activity thanks to the continuing railroad traffic. The R. E. Bridges business, which succeeded John Buck Company, was one of three general stores operating in a community with a population of about 100. (Courtesy of Jackson County Historical Society.)

As the downtown business district grew north along what is now Main Street, the town's lone bank provided services to a community that included at least 12 fruit growers in and around Makanda. (Courtesy of Jackson County Historical Society.)

J. W. Carr's was one of three general stores operating in Makanda in the late 1800s, seen here along the east side of Main Street, according to an account in 1893 from the *Illinois State Gazetteer*. (Courtesy of Jackson County Historical Society.)

As Makanda's fruit interests grew, so did its boardwalk. According to U.S. Census Bureau information from 2007, the small community had 29 businesses with 190 employees. (Courtesy of Jackson County Historical Society.)

Makanda's neighbor to the north, Boskeydell, saw its Illinois Central Railroad depot finished in 1857 as well. Marketing its strong points, the town prided itself on sitting reasonably close to the bustling big cities of Chicago and New Orleans. (Courtesy of Jackson County Historical Society.)

During its heyday as a fruit producer, Makanda and its downtown area would play host to hundreds of growers and workers eager to load goods for shipment north to Chicago.

Visit us at
arcadiapublishing.com

www.ingramcontent.com/pod-product-compliance
Lightning Source LLC
Chambersburg PA
CBHW050625110426
42813CB00007B/1721